Ramsay Richard Reinagle: John Constable, *1799 (detail) - Oil on canvas - London, National Portrait Gallery.*

CONSTABLE

"The sound of water escaping from mill dams, willows, old rotten planks, slimy posts and brickwork - I love such things. These things made me a painter and I am grateful."

John Constable

Constable and Turner, the two greatest landscape painters of Britain, were almost exact contemporaries, but their ways of painting, their personalities and their lives could hardly have been more different. Turner, a lifelong Londoner who travelled widely abroad, achieved success early in life through emulating and even surpassing the great masters of the past; his canvases glow gold with all the colours of the sky, red with sunsets, fire, storms and inhuman splendours. Constable, by contrast, never left England. He was so rooted in his own corner of Suffolk that its images of trees, clouds and waterways hardly ever left him. He struggled to achieve in late middle age the recognition (full Royal Academy membership) which Turner gained in his twenties.

John Constable was born in East Bergholt, Suffolk, on the 11th July, 1776 "in the fertile valley of the Stour, which marks the southern boundary of the county with Essex." His father was a prosperous entrepreneur who built up a profitable barge transport business on the Stour. Such provincial prosperity, however, was of little use to Constable as a painter. To win recognition in London he had to become a member of the Royal Academy - the most important artistic society in Britain.

In 1798, at the age of 22, he went to London and enrolled as a student at the Academy. There he received advice and encouragement from Joseph Farington, a well-known art lover with important connections. Constable exhibited some of his earliest derivative works - often classical nude studies - at the Academy and came to realise that for him painting was to be a calling, not a hobby. Yet, unusually, he decided to leave London and return to East Bergholt, his birthplace.

He wanted to paint nature just as he saw it, without any models or undue external influences. He did not approve of the easy solutions being adopted by fashionable landscape painters, whom he accused of "running after pictures and seeking the truth at second hand". Nor did he think much of the taste for obviously "picturesque" subjects, such as ruined abbeys or moonlit castles, then so popular and painted by successful painters like Thomas Girtin.

Constable returned to Suffolk in 1802 and his father gave him a studio near the Constable home. In it, over the years, he laboriously worked out his own individual style

Old Sarum *circa 1832 - watercolour 30.1 x 48.6 cm - London, Victoria and Albert Museum*

of painting. He wanted above all to be true to himself; his paintings are approachable, pleasant and honest. Almost always, at least until near the end of his life, Constable preferred to paint populated, well-tended landscapes, such as *Flatford Mill* (page 8) rather than the stormy, melodramatic landscapes or paintings inspired by literary sources. The subjects of his paintings are very simple, being that which he saw around him in everyday life. He was never afraid of being thought dull or unheroic in academic circles, where historical or biblical themes were preferred. In this respect he was closer to the lesser Dutch masters of the 17th

century who had celebrated everyday life and humble occupations, than to the grandiose themes of the popular Italian or French masters like Claude Lorrain or Poussin.

Constable briefly visited the Lake District in 1806 and, more importantly, Salisbury where he stayed at the home of its archdeacon (later its bishop) John Fisher, who became a close friend. He painted its cathedral several times (page 18). The cathedral was more than just a fine subject to Constable; it symbolised to him the almost mystical union of the Church of England with the English landscape. Constable remained profoundly conservative all his life, rejecting both current "improvements" in agriculture and liberal measures in politics, such as emancipating Catholics. In this he shared the views of his contemporary, Jane Austen.

Although East Bergholt remained his favourite place, where he devoted much time, particularly in summer and autumn, to the study of his beloved Suffolk landscape, he could never forget that his fortune would be decided in London with admission to the Royal Academy. This was why he accepted all commissions for portraits (even copying other paint-

Stonehenge *1836 - watercolour 38.7 x 59 cm - London, Victoria and Albert Museum*

ings) and why he tried to exhibit a landscape every year at the Royal Academy. He was finally made an Associate of the Academy in 1819 and a full member only in 1829.

However, meticulous observation of the beauty of Suffolk, which did not preclude a strongly sentimental touch, remained his keynote. It took Constable many years of quiet self-apprenticeship and experiment before he could combine all his detailed studies successfully into major paintings. His earliest successful canvases of about 1814, such as *Golding Constable's Kitchen Garden* chose unfashionably humble subjects but impressed a few of the more perceptive local critics. All this was to change for him around the time of his fortieth birthday.

Constable had fallen in love with a girl in his village, Maria Bicknell, in 1808. She returned his love but her important and wealthy family would not let her marry a penniless, unsuccessful painter. In 1816 the death of his father left Constable fairly well-off and he finally married Maria in 1816, honeymooning in Dorset, where he painted one of his first beach scenes *Weymouth Bay* (page 6). Constable now settled in London. Driven perhaps by the need to provide for a growing family, he began to paint far more copiously. He returned to East Anglia only for occasional visits, but the memories of his Suffolk years were the essence of the landscapes which were to make him famous. (In fact, these years were ones of acute agrarian unrest, with hayricks being burnt by rioting workless labourers and mounting social tension; but Constable resolutely ignored such threats). He now began to exhibit what he called his six-footers - large, highly finished canvases, such as *Flatford Mill* (page 8) and, in 1819, *The White Horse*, which was well received by critics, some of them even comparing it favourably with the generally more esteemed works of Turner.

In 1824, Constable moved to Brighton to try to help his wife's tuberculosis. Here he painted a series of seascapes, such as *Brighton Beach* (page 20) and *The Chain Pier, Brighton* (page 24) but he never shared Turner's obsession with the sea. The artist was now travelling between Brighton, London and Hampstead, where in the early 1820s he did his most interesting series of cloud studies (page 16). The subject of these studies were fragments of sky, clouds and trees, and the effects of weather conditions, the changing light and the wind. Two years later he moved his family permanently to Hampstead, then outside London. Having just given birth to her seventh child, his adored wife died in November 1828 - from exhaustion and tuberculosis. Constable was left in a state of near-total despair and solitude.

From then on, he became increasingly gloomy and his work at times reflected this, as in his desolate view of *Stonehenge* (page 2). Storms predominate in his later work. In *Salisbury Cathedral From The Meadows*, painted in 1830-31, the gloomy atmosphere and the iridescent brilliance of the rainbow are rich in symbolic meanings. He wrote to Charles Leslie on 15 December 1834, three years before his sudden death (probably from a heart attack): "... Every hint of joy in art has been reduced to a minimum for me; is it therefore surprising that I should always paint storms? Storm after storm until darkness takes over ..."

View of Hedingham Castle, Essex circa 1802 - ink sketch - Private Collection

Windsor Castle From The River 1802 - watercolour sketch - London, Victoria and Albert Museum

LANDSCAPE AND DOUBLE RAINBOW

1812 - Oil on paper stuck to canvas, 33.7 x 38.4 cm
London, Victoria and Albert Museum.

One of Constable's greatest strengths was his skill in depicting the constantly changing light and colour of the sky. In the following landscapes, a small detail of the sky is featured, demonstrating Constable's confident handling of this difficult subject. Here the sky, which fills practically the whole canvas, is illuminated by the colours of the double rainbow.

This painting by Constable, done just as he was finally finding his true style, recalls the oils and watercolours on the same subject by William Turner (1775-1851). Turner aimed to represent light and its iridescent effects upon the landscape, over the years developing and perfecting this approach to such an extent that realistic features in his later works are dissolved into pure colour. Constable's style was completely different. It was a totally natural vision that triumphed in his paintings. His aim was to reproduce the most tangible and familiar aspects of a landscape: light moving across fields and touching the leaves of trees, clear skies and the glow of a summer's day. He achieved this through constant, meticulously detailed study of the real world. He also came to rely very heavily upon a series of drawings and coloured sketches in oils (this was unusual - most painters preferred to sketch in watercolours or charcoal) that he would put aside and then take up and re-work years later. Such a method suited his hesitant style, which took many years to mature sufficiently to win recognition outside his own circle. Despite their perfection, many of his finished canvases lack the immediacy of these oil sketches.

Joseph Mallard William Turner - Buttermere Lake with Part of Cromackwater, Cumberland, A Shower, *1789 - Oil on canvas, 91.5 x 122 cm - London, Tate Gallery. The magical effect of light forms the basis of the sensation of space in Turner's paintings.*

WEYMOUTH BAY

1816 - Oil on wood, 20.3 x 24.7 cm
London, Victoria and Albert Museum

Constable used large strokes of his spatula to "construct" the mass of clouds that come up from behind the hill and appear to bowl towards us. He spread out his colours - white, ochre, blue and grey - against the blue of the sky. The effect is both evocative and immediate.

Constable was not fond of seascapes, but he admired this particular part of the Dorset coast which he saw on his honeymoon in 1816. This painting of Weymouth Bay is not in fact a seascape in the usual sense, for the sea is relegated to a small, rather unimpressive strip of water on the left. What fills the foreground and centre of the picture is the immense reddish-brown expanse of the beach, whose almost earthy tones are repeated on the hilltop in the background and echoed by the cliffs on the right. Racing along above the bay, the huge rolling clouds emphasise again that almost always in a Constable landscape, it is the sky which dominates his paintings.

There is a typical underlying honesty to unidealised landscapes such as this. Constable was deeply inspired by his slightly older contemporary William Wordsworth, the great Romantic poet of landscape whose belief in honesty of vision Constable in many ways shared. Both men reacted against the 18th century convention that only a few subjects, usually chosen from classical or biblical sources, were suitable for either poetry or paint-

ing. Instead they looked around them at their native country - wild, rather dour Cumbrian mountains in Wordsworth's case; lush fertile Suffolk valleys in Constable's - with their unheroic, hard-working inhabitants for their subjects and discarded even superficial references to biblical or classical themes, as in *Weymouth Bay*.

Thomas Barker (1769 - 1847) The Countryside Near Bath, Oil on canvas, 80 x 105 cm - London, Tate Gallery. This picture confirms the influence of Dutch painting, which chose everyday unheroic subjects, on English 18th and 19th century painting and echoes the composition of Constable's Weymouth Bay.

Constable used a full brush to reinforce the images on the canvas, whether they were waves breaking on the pebbled beach (1) or the blue tinted clouds in the sky (2).

" **...I**f an artist insists on working without reference to nature
he will inevitably become mannered .."

John Constable

FLATFORD MILL

1817 - Oil on canvas, 102 x 127 cm
London, Tate Gallery

The serenity of the landscape is reflected in the soft, broken outline of the clouds which seem to be made of cotton wool, in the grey-blue sky receding behind the red brick houses and in the bright green of the trees.

Flatford Mill was one of Constable's great series of large paintings on the beauties of Suffolk, its fields, canals, woods and rivers; he called them his "six-footers" although in fact few of them measured exactly six feet in reality.

While Turner was travelling all round Europe looking for pictorial excitement, Constable kept returning to the same scenes all within a few miles of one another. As he said, "My limited and restricted art may be found under every hedge". The painting was exhibited in 1817 under the title *Scene On A Navigable River Or Flatford Mill*. The painting depicts a peaceful summer landscape, opening to the right onto a sun and shade dappled field; the smoke rising almost vertically from the house in the distance indicates that there is very little wind. The mill was one of several belonging to Constable's father, Golding Constable; it is now a centre for nature studies.

Englefield House, 1832 - London, Victoria and Albert Museum. A watercolour sketch made at the height of Constable's career. The sketch confirms the artist's capacity for composition, which was unaffected by the use of a different medium. In the sketch he realises his aim of reproducing the phenomena of light and shade in nature, accentuating its infinite beauty and admirable power of expression.

Below: Two details from the painting on the previous page. In the first, the boy's body tenses under the strain of pushing the heavy boat with a long pole. The other shows a child on horseback, turning to speak to his companion. Both show Constable capable of portraying people as well as nature.

Near Stoke-by-Nayland, 1807 - Oil on canvas, 33.5 x 44.5 cm - London, Tate Gallery

A SKETCH IN OILS
Before he painted his large canvases Constable would make many sketches in order to clarify his ideas. These preparatory sketches took several forms: some were studies in pencil, some were life drawings and others were executed on a grand scale, using oils to capture the complexity of both the foreground and the background.
This oil sketch has freshness and immediacy. Not many colours are used. Constable's palette was based on yellow (the natural colour of baked earth), green and blue. In this rough sketch the brush strokes stand out clearly, running diagonally from left to right. It is possible to identify the different stages of the sketch. A first tentative pencil outline fixes the position of the relatively low horizon. The composition consists of a building in the background to the left, whilst the foreground is occupied by trees massed along the diagonal. The blotches of colour are made up of a mixture of greens and browns and large, broken brushstrokes of blue. Finally, the luminous white of the clouds, the facade of the house to the left and the dress of the girl with the umbrella stand out from the background together with the yellow of the bushes and the earth in the foreground on the right.

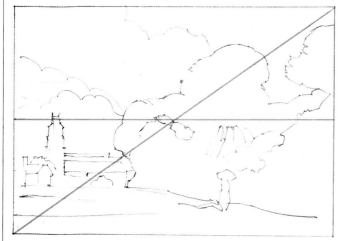

This painting, conventional enough in showing a rural scene (much painted by Dutch masters such as Van Goyen in the 17th century), shows clearly Constable's originality and burgeoning genius in his drawing and painting of trees, the varied shapes of their trunks, the variety of their colours, above all perhaps in the transparency of the light and in the reflections of the shadows. The ochre colours of the earth, the delicate greens of the field, the brilliant green leaves on the great trees, the red bricks of the mill and the blue and greys of the cloudy sky combine to create an extraordinary harmony of colour. Constable is particularly adept at showing the very English sort of rather gentle, undramatic, shade and light in the shadows cast by the trees. In his letters he talked frequently about "the chiaroscuro of nature" by which he meant something less dramatic than an Italian painter would have done but which had for him a moral significance. He referred to his landscapes as always being concerned with "morality"; although far from preaching to us, his great land-scapes have a message of the good life - simple yet noble - in the country. Such sentiments derive from his High Tory (ultra-conservative) beliefs in the traditional social structure. Wheeling soundlessly high above the human and natural landscape, the great grey-white mass of cumulus cloud reflects another enduring element in Constable's works - cloud studies, the importance of which was to increase for him from this time on. East Anglia is of course famous for its great cloudscapes.

MRS ANDREW

1818 - Oil on canvas, 63 x 76 cm
London, Tate Gallery

In Constable's day portrait painting represented one of the principal sources of income for English painters. Paintings with historical, classical and biblical themes were also very popular, as Turner's career showed; landscapes were definitely a less prestigious and so less lucrative art form. It was natural that Constable, whilst making his way as a landscape painter, should also seek to make his name as a portraitist (he also painted several altar pieces). Yet nature continued to be his chief source of inspiration. He only found portrait painting satisfying if he was linked to his subject by friendship, love or some other tie. The portrait of Mrs Andrew makes a pair with the painting of her husband, Doctor James Andrew of Addiscombe College, whom he knew well. It was one of Constable's last commissioned portraits and one of his best. It is notable for the composed dignity of the sitter, so unlike the flattering, rather showy portraits by Sir Thomas Lawrence, the leading portrait painter of fashionable society who was about to become President of the Royal Academy. This is certainly not an idealised portrait. Its "classical" composition is

John Charles Constable, 1824/25 - Oil on canvas - Private collection. In this painting of his eldest son Constable does not miss the opportunity of painting a landscape beyond the child's shoulders. He has captured the boy in a quiet moment during a game. He stands at the centre of the canvas surrounded by his favourite toys - a hoop in his hands and a drum at his feet. The paving slabs beneath his feet are represented by lines in perfect perspective that look rather like a stage set. The painting is another proof of Constable's ability to paint portraits.

striking, based on the form of the pyramid that "blocks out" the figure. The transparent whites of the dress and bonnet contrast with her face, framed by her dark hair.

This sketch of two of the artist's children is executed in ink and watercolours. The children have made themselves a carriage out of two upturned chairs and a wooden horse is pulling them. The sketch conveys the sense of a fleeting moment, caught and dashed down on paper. The drawing reveals the artist's deep affection for his children.

TREES AT HAMPSTEAD

1821 - Oil on canvas, 91.5 x 72.5 cm
London, Victoria and Albert Museum

Clouds move behind the line of trees and fill up the whole sky. The colour of the sky causes the branches and leaves to stand out sharply in silhouette.

Like every other landscape painter, Constable was fascinated by trees. Structure and balance, besides their evident beauty, are undoubtedly the qualities that draw artists towards trees as subjects, observing the shape of the trunk as it gives way to the branches and then the slow multiplication of those branches. Whether obvious or not, this process always follows a law and a logic of its own. Constable did not consider trees as mere elements of the landscape. He studied the unique character of each tree which he painted, often including its complex design and rich structure in the foreground. His studies of elms and willows are particularly fine.

In 1819 Constable rented his first house in Hampstead, hoping that its location high up outside London would prove beneficial to the health of his tubercular wife Maria. Years later he was to take up permanent residence there. Thus Hampstead, its hills, trees, clouds and skies became the subject of numerous paintings. The artist made an accurate note of the time, date and weather conditions on the back of each picture. He was seeking to establish the relationship between the quality of the light and the cloudiness or clearness of the sky. Constable was one of the first painters of the period to work in the "suburbs", combining the themes of houses, trees and nature.

Constable found in Hampstead, already a popular suburb, the same domesticated or humanised landscape he had known in Suffolk.

Group of trees, landscape and cloud study - *Black pencil and white lead on light brown paper, 27.5 x 36.2 cm - Florence, Horne Museum. This is a typically vivid sketch.*

Claude-Oscar Monet: Poplars On The Epte, 1891 - Oil on canvas, 90 x 70 cm - Private collection. Both Constable and Monet sought to represent in their paintings light and the luminosity of both colour and atmosphere. It is interesting to notice the difference between their interpretations of trees and sky. Monet's bright colour and rapid brushstrokes show up by contrast the accurate tracery of leaves in Constable's painting. Despite the warm colours of the French painter, his calm approach to painting is very different from that of the passionate Englishman.

CIRRUS CLOUDS

c. 1821- Oil on paper 11.4 x 17.8 cm London, Victoria and Albert Museum

Using thick, heavy brushstrokes and oil paint, Constable was able to capture the ever-changing shapes of the clouds. This sketch is a particularly fine example of his vision and technique.

This is a masterpiece amongst Constable's many sketches, capturing a fleeting moment with rapid strokes of the brush. Anyone who has paused to watch the sky, seeing the clouds rushing along, chasing each other, joining together, dividing, and taking on the forms of animals, castles or soft mountains of foam, can imagine how difficult it is to paint this constantly changing spectacle. Constable's sketch succeeds in conveying the movements of the clouds, the transparency of the atmosphere and the depth of the sky. Seeing the sketch as a "scrap of sky", cut out of infinity, without boundaries, with neither foreground nor perspective, it becomes particularly difficult to grasp. It is based purely on colour and subtle brushstrokes. The sketch conveys the wind, which seems to carry the clouds higher, out of the painting and into the infinity of the sky. As he himself said, "The landscape painter who does not make the skies a very material part of his composition - neglects to avail himself of one of his greatest aids ... I have often been advised to consider my sky as a 'white sheet drawn behind the objects'. Certainly, if the sky is obtrusive as mine are, it is bad, but if they are evaded (as mine are not) it is worse, they must and always shall with me make an effectual part of the composition. It will be difficult to name a class of landscape in which the sky is not the keynote ... and the chief organ of sentiment. The sky is the source of light in nature and it governs everything."

The paintings that were based on these sketches appear to represent Constable at the height of his maturity as a painter. However, these large-scale drawings from life are far more evocative than the finished works.
Study Of Sky And Trees (above), and A Storm At Sunset (below), both in the Victoria and Albert Museum, London.

" I shall shortly return to Bergholt where I shall make some laborious studies from nature. I shall endeavour to get a pure, unaffected representation of the scenes that may employ me with respect to colour or anything else. Drawing I am pretty well master of."

John Constable, June 1802

SALISBURY CATHEDRAL FROM THE BISHOP'S GROUNDS

1823 - Oil on canvas, 87.6 x 111.8 cm
London, Victoria and Albert Museum

The lyricism of this painting derives from its vividly blue sky, the white clouds against which the cathedral spire stands out, and the shape made by the branches of the trees which frame the cathedral in a way not unlike a gothic arch.

This canvas is a working-up of a sketch Constable had first made as far back as 1811 - a practice typical of him. There is an obvious link between the slender, elegant outline of the cathedral and the two bending elm trees in the foreground which frame it like a suitably Gothic arch. This probably reflects the idea, common at the time, that Gothic architecture evolved in imitation of the groves where the worship of nature had once been conducted. The Church of England was accordingly the natural church for a still mainly rural England, epitomised by the cattle grazing contentedly in the meadows in the middle ground. John Fisher, Constable's great friend and supporter throughout his life, was bishop (previously archdeacon) of Salisbury. The painting emphasises the unity of the Church of England, English society and the natural world. But Constable was far too great a painter to allow his politics to intrude obviously on his art, even though the picture was commissioned by Bishop Fisher.

The transparency, depth, atmosphere and pictorial effectiveness of this painting of the Cathedral are not matched by his later versions. The reasons for this are complex, but without doubt the increasing depression felt by Constable after his wife's death in 1828 contributed to the darker, more sinister tones of the 1831 version.

Salisbury Cathedral From The River - *1820 Oil on canvas, 52.7 x 76.8 cm - London, National Gallery. This large oil sketch is based on two basic colours, ochre and green which complement each other and blend together in the meadow, the foliage of the trees and spire. The colours blend to grow darker in the river, lighter in the sky.*

BRIGHTON BEACH

1824 - Oil on paper, 13.6 x 30.2 cm
London, Victoria and Albert Museum

More clouds, like a white transparent veil partially covering the ochre hues of an autumn sky, above the blue-green sea which is edged by the warm ochre of the sand in the foreground.

Constable's style slowly developed from the serenity and tonal harmony of his early years to what he called "the chiaroscuro of nature". By this he meant the play of light which throws rays of colour onto shaded areas, making rain-drenched leaves shimmer in the sun and outlining the movement of the clouds in the sky.

His time in Brighton - a resort which had little appeal to him but whose bracing air would, it was vainly hoped, help his wife's tuberculosis, this being the age when the virtues of sea air or even sea water were all the rage - came at the early stages of this transformation. Constable never came to enjoy painting the sea as much as the land or sky - unlike Turner - but, as he had it there to paint, he set to work with his customary determination. Seascapes, anyway, demanded a new approach, with their essentially fluid forms and brighter colours. His method of painting accordingly became more direct, so that he could fix the fast-moving image onto the canvas. He had to use a spatula to apply the paint as fast as possible. Then he would use a loaded brush later to add texture to the water, the trees, the fields or the beach and the sky.

It is a simple composition. Its fascination and suggestive power lie in the skilled layering of the various planes of perspective, in the diagonal slant of the sea-edge, in the seething waves and the movement of the clouds. The juxtaposition of the colours of the sky, the sea and the beach is equally dramatic.

Opposite left: David Cox - The Strand At Rhyl,
1834/35 - Oil on canvas, 74 x 135 cm -
Birmingham, City Museum and Art Gallery. This
painting has the same components as in Constable's
Brighton Beach. Here there is the added detail of the
wind sweeping the beach, blowing the ladies'
clothes and driving the clouds through the autumnal
light. Cox became famous for his watercolours and
storm scenes and he produced some remarkable
works such as this beautiful coastal scene.
J. M. W. Turner - The Beach At Calais At Low Tide,
Women Gathering Mussels, 1830 - Oil on canvas
73 x 107 cm - Bury St Edmunds, Art Gallery and
Museum. When he painted seascapes such as this
Turner also used pencil-drawn sketches taken from
life. These he would then transform into a dramatic
symphony of light and colour.

THE CORNFIELD

1826 - Oil on canvas, 142 x 122 cm
London, National Gallery

The whites and transparent blues of the clouds and sky are important to the painting, a composition which leads along the path to the edge of the field and beyond.

This painting, exhibited in 1826, deliberately looks back to the picturesque tradition Constable had earlier rejected, in particular to Gainsborough. It contained, said Constable dismissively, "a little more eyesalve than I normally condescend to give them" - them in this instance being the picture-buying public, to whom he hoped to sell it. Several things reveal how far Constable had pandered to the often uncomprehending tastes of his viewers in this painting. There are explicit references to Gainsborough's works: the track and pond have their origins in Gainsborough's Cornard Wood. The dead tree on the left also looks to Gainsborough and the Picturesque style in particular. No decent farmer would have sown wheat right up to the stream's edge, for it would have been impossible to harvest. Nor would a shepherd boy (seen left, drinking from the stream) have let his flock amble on towards a gate open into a field of ripe corn. Despite such concessions to his public, Constable has not in fact changed his style that much. Constable reworked this from an earlier sketch as was his custom, studying the same subject on more than one occasion. He would use a different viewpoint as he tried to find the best balance in the composition. He would also make sketches at different times of day, recording the variations in light, so as to find the most evocative. Constable relied heavily on his memories of this path which led across the fields from East Bergholt to Dedham.

Thomas Gainsborough Gainsborough Forest (Cornard Wood), 1748 - Oil on canvas, 120 x 150 cm - London, National Gallery. Gainsborough was a strong early influence on Constable, even though Constable later rejected the older artist's style as too picturesque. Here, however, the ultimate source for The Cornfield is clearly Gainsborough, in composition as well as spirit.

John Sell Cotman - The Stage Coach - Oil on board, 41 x 35 cm - Norwich, Castle Museum. Cotman (1782-1842) was a member of the Norwich School of landscape painters which flourished in the early 19th century. This painting by him is also dominated by trees. The coach plays an important part in the picture. The striking red figure of the horseman stands out against the pleasing juxtaposition of the yellow-green hues of the trees and the blues of the distant background.

THE CHAIN PIER

1827 - Oil on canvas, 127 x 182 cm
London, Tate Gallery

Few painters have succeeded as well as Constable has here in so perfectly conveying the brilliance of the atmosphere seen through the rain, as well as the crashing of the waves and the howling of the wind.

Constable did not much like Brighton which he found vulgar, although he acknowledged "its wonderful air for setting people up". However, he clearly was willing to attempt seascapes - perhaps in an attempt to rival Turner.

The effect of light and shade in the clouds and sea has been brilliantly rendered here. The composition is based on the line of the low-lying horizon, with the sky and swiftly advancing clouds occupying two-thirds of the canvas. The distant outlines of the houses and the Chain Pier appear in the background. There are several boats in the foreground on the left, one with a yellow sail, while the fishermen along the diagonal line of the sea edge add to the scene's movement. The effect of rain threatening is conveyed by the various tones of the two basic colours in the painting: the ochre of the sea-edge, the boats and the houses, and the blue of the sky and the sea, which is enlivened by the yellow and white patches of the sails. It is against the background of these basic colours that Constable has carefully arranged the details of baskets, anchors, poles, hulls and sand, as well as the crests of the waves. The three-dimensional quality of the clouds gives them the impression of rolling massively towards us. This is one of his most vivid works.

Sir August Wall Callcott: Coastal View, With Mole, c 1834 - Oil on canvas, 70 x 89 cm - London, Tate Gallery. This artist was mainly influenced by Italian tradition, both in his landscapes and his marine painting. He was as famous as Turner in his time. This painting, like Constable's Chain Pier, shows a low-lying horizon giving much space to the cloudy sky. The light from the left of the painting throws the shadows of the characters onto the jetty.

THE GLEBE FARM

1827 - Oil on board, 59.7 x 78.1 cm
London, Tate Gallery

For this painting so rooted in the past, Constable decided to paint a serene sky dotted with light clouds perhaps suggesting the transience of all earthly things.

This picture was intended as a memorial to his old friend and mentor, John Fisher, Bishop of Salisbury, who had died in 1825. This glebe (land attached to a parish church) had formed part of Fisher's first living as a clergyman. The close relationship of farm and church (visible on the right) was meant to symbolise once again the old Tory concept of a link between the established Church and the countryside. There is an undertone of suitable melancholy about the entire picture, for the rich vegetation surrounding the Glebe house is heavy, even dark.

It remains a most impressive work and Constable later wrote of it, "This is one of the pictures on which I rest my few pretensions to futurity". His skilful handling of colour gives an impression of a breeze moving through the branches. The hedges and paths disappear into the distance through the shimmering atmosphere, while the clouds change colour and break up.

The words of Eugène Delacroix, one of Constable's greatest admirers in France, are revealing: "Constable says the superiority of the greens of his fields is because it is made up of an infinite variety of greens. The lack of intensity and life in the greens used by most landscape painters is because most of them make their greens uniform. What I have just said about green applies also to other colours".

It is interesting to compare the oil sketch (shown above) painted from life with the definitive painting produced in the studio. In spite of the greater precision in drawing the shapes and details and the more sophisticated techniques used by the artist, the finished work has lost much of the moving quality of the study. It no longer has the freshness and immediacy of a scene painted from life.

BRANCH HILL POND

1828 - Oil on canvas, 59.6 x 77.6 cm
London, Victoria and Albert Museum

All Constable's experience and cloud studies are brought into play in the sky of Branch Hill Pond. The artist has built up the whirling cloud effects by applying white paint with a spatula to the base tone of the sky. Once again the sky takes up half the canvas and is the overwhelmingly dominant element.

This is one of a great number of sketches and finished paintings Constable did of this part of Hampstead Heath. He walked regularly, sketching and observing around Branch Hill Pond. The Heath's landscape and skies provided the subject-matter for many of his later works.

For Constable, space only existed as a definition of its components. He rendered it with patches of colour applied to the canvas quickly with large brushstrokes or with a spatula. Turner, however, transformed any actual space into a sort of universal space, dominated by immense forces which absorbed every object to the point of dissolving trees and buildings into mere spirals of air and flashes of light. This does not mean that Constable should be thought of as a mere topographer. The image perceived by any individual sends forth impressions and sensations; these Constable interpreted and transferred into his own pictorial sense, reflecting his often intense emotion. In *Branch Hill Pond* (of which several other versions exist in the Victoria and Albert Museum and the Tate Gallery) the finished painting has preserved the qualities of his more spontaneous, quick sketches unusually well.

Indeed, few of his oil sketches are so impressionistic in style as *Branch Hill Pond*. However Constable was very different from the later generation of French painters in his emotional involvement. Constable was a true Romantic, his works always marked by deep emotion.

Above left: Claude Lorrain - Lake Near
Rome, c. 1640 - London, British Museum.
Below left: Thomas Gainsborough (1727-
1788) - Landscape With Bridge
London, Tate Gallery.
Both Claude and Gainsborough greatly
influenced all the landscape painters of
Constable's time, and both produced
landscapes which were in some ways
idealised. Constable himself said that, "In
Claude's landscape all is lovely, all
amiable, all is amenity and repose; the
calm sunshine of the heart. He carried
landscape to perfection, that is, human
perfection". But Constable never tried to
emulate or surpass Claude as Turner did, for
his vision was fundamentally different -
unidealised if not unsentimental.
Gainsborough was a far closer influence -
in space, time and feeling. Constable said
of him, "The landscape of Gainsborough is
soothing, tender and affecting. The stillness
of noon, the depths of twilight and the dew
of pearls of the morning are all to be found
on the canvases of this most benevolent and
kind-hearted man."

A TRUE ENGLISH PAINTER

Constable's techniques make him seem in some ways a forerunner of the Impressionists. His love for nature led him to work from life. He used whites, yellows, blues and reds in their pure state and he recognised the importance of changing light and its effect on the landscape. These give an unexpectedly modern quality to his paintings, studies, sketches and drawings. But they are also full of the deep emotional resonances which make him a true painter of his Romantic age.

His subjects began with pictures of his birthplace. He made paintings of his father's house, Dedham Vale, the dyke and mill at Flatford, the Stour, the clear dawns and the sunsets of Suffolk summer evenings, and the churches of East Bergholt, Stratford St Mary and Stoke by Nayland. These were views with strong emotional associations for him, stemming from his long familiarity with them. In the years around 1810 Constable's art finally acquired a definite character of its own, after a long and uncertain period of false starts, imitations and laborious studies.

From an initially dramatic style with tense, contrasting colours, his pictures came to have a gentler, more subtle expressiveness by which places full of memories were rendered by flowing brush strokes and toned-down colours. In this East Bergholt period Constable first began to make detailed studies of the horses, carts, ploughs and flowers which he would incorporate into his great compositions.

Then came the first of the large canvases in which Constable depicted everyday scenes in a realistic way. *Flatford Mill* (pages 8-11) was exhibited in 1817; it incorporates the distilled essence of

CONSTABLE AND HIS TIMES

	HIS LIFE AND WORKS	HISTORY	ART AND CULTURE
1776	Born 11 July at East Bergholt, Suffolk, son of a wealthy mill-owner	Declaration of Independence by the United States; beginning of the American War of Independence	Jean-Jacques Rousseau: *Reveries* Edward Gibbon: *Decline And Fall Of The Roman Empire (vol 1)* Death of David Hume
1799	Studies in London at the Royal Academy	Napoleon Bonaparte seizes power Income tax introduced in England Combination Acts against trade unions	Death of Beaumarchais Parker invents cement
1802	Exhibits for the first time at the Royal Academy	Napoleon is made First Consul for life in France Peace of Amiens between France and Britain (lasting 13 months)	Elgin Marbles brought to London from Athenian Acropolis by Lord Elgin Beethoven: *Kreutzer Sonata*
1806	Makes a journey to the Lake District where he does numerous watercolours and oil sketches	Death of Prime Minister William Pitt; succeeded by Greville's short-lived "All-Talents" Ministry Prohibition of Slave Trade in British Empire	Birth of Elizabeth Browning and J.S. Mill Death of J.H.Fragonard
1815	Exhibits *Boat Building Near Flatford* at the Royal Academy. Death of his mother	The Hundred Days; Napoleon returns to France but is defeated at Waterloo Congress of Vienna	P. B. Shelley: *Alastor* Birth of Anthony Trollope
1816	Death of his father. Marries Maria Bicknell after seven years of opposition from her family	Spa Field riots in London Argentina declares independence	Lord Byron: *Childe Harold's Pilgrimage (Canto III)* S. T. Coleridge: *Cristabel* Birth of Charlotte Brontë
1817	Birth of his first son John Charles	End of Serbian revolt against Turks Derbyshire rising suppressed	Mary Wollstonecraft Shelley: *Frankenstein* Death of Jane Austen
1819	Exhibits *The White Horse* at the Royal Academy. Birth of daughter Maria. Elected Associate of the Royal Academy after repeated applications	Peterloo massacre in Manchester; troops charge crowd Six Acts passed to limit political freedom in Britain	John Keats: *Ode To A Nightingale* Byron starts publication of first cantos of *Don Juan*

his previous studies, even though its unity of composition is not as perfect as in his later large canvases. The colours depicting reality are pure but the excessive attention paid to detail combined with his first attempt at a very large canvas (101.7 x 127 cm) have resulted in the perspective becoming in places confused.

The White Horse, exhibited at the Royal Academy two years later, was better conceived. The painting is even larger than the previous one, but the composition is well-balanced. It shows a rural landscape in undramatic colours, both realistic and sentimental at the same time. "I shall never cease to paint such scenes, which have always attracted me...I should paint my own places best. Painting is but another word for feeling." This letter to his friend John Fisher, was dated 23 October 1821. By then, he had left definitely Suffolk to move between Hampstead, London and Brighton.

This parting had happened in the crucial year when he went with his new wife to live in London in 1816. Since then he had made a series of paintings of Salisbury Cathedral and the surrounding countryside. He had also come to know Hampstead with its views over the Heath. Here he felt less emotionally involved with the landscape than in Suffolk, and he moved away from depicting a particular locality. Instead he turned his attention to small, individual details such as trees, sky and clouds in particular weather conditions, and the changes in their shape and colour during the course of the day.

The notes on the back of these small studies are all identical in format and they show Constable's accurate, systematic way of working. This was similar to the

1821	Exhibits *The Hay Wain* at the Royal Academy. Series of studies clouds on Hampstead Heath	Beginning of the Greek revolt against the Turks arouses great sympathy in the West; rebellions also in Moldavia and Wallachia	Death of John Keats P. B. Shelley: *Adonais* John Nash starts building Regent's Terrace
1824	Exhibits *The Hay Wain* at the Paris Salon where it wins a gold medal. Constable is now more famous in France than in England	Repeal of the Combination Acts against trade unions Charles X succeeds Louis XVIII in France and introduces reactionary measure	Eugène Delacroix exhibits *The Massacre of Chios* after being influenced by Constable Death of Byron in Messalonghi and of Géricault
1825	Exhibits *The Leaping Horse* at the Royal Academy	Amending Acts restrict union power In Russia, Decembrist rising against new Czar Nicolas I savagely crushed	Pushkin writes *Boris Godunov* Death of J. H. Fuseli
1828	His wife dies of TB; Constable overwhelmed with grief	Wellington becomes Prime Minister Repeal of the Tests and Corporations Act emancipates non-conforming protestants	Victor Hugo: *Songs And Ballads* Death of Goya Birth of Tolstoy Turner painting at Petworth
1829	Exhibits *Hadleigh Castle*. Elected full member of the Royal Academy	Robert Peel founds the Metropolitan Police Catholic Relief Act emancipates Catholics	Giacomo Leopardi: *Peace After The Storm* Edgar Allan Poe: *El Araaf*
1830	Publishes a series of engravings called *English Landscapes*, which proves a failure and costs him his wife's inheritance	William IV comes to throne of England Seizure of Algiers by the French Earl Grey becomes Prime Minister, heading new reformist administration	Chopin: Two Piano Concertos Stendhal: *The Scarlet And The Black*
1836	Delivers series of lectures on *The History Of Landscape*	Liberal ministry of Lord Melbourne Louis-Napoleon (nephew of Napoleon Bonaparte) fails in attempt to overthrow French government	Alphonse de Musset: *Confessions* Augustus Pugin: *Contrasts (first edition)*
1837	Dies in London 31 March, probably from a heart attack	Victoria comes to the throne Morse invents the telegraph	Thomas Carlyle: *The French Revolution* Charles Barry builds the Reform Club Death of Leopardi

Impressionists' approach, where a more poetic note was added to the painting's scientific analysis. An example of these notes describes a study of clouds and trees as follows: "Hampstead, 11 September 1821. From 10 to 11 in the morning in the sun. Silver-grey clouds against a background of oppressive heat. Light south-east wind, beautiful weather throughout the day, but rain at night." Again, written on a study of skies and trees with a red house: "12 September 1821. Noon. Wind fresh at West. Sun very hot. Looking southward, exceedingly bright, vivid and glowing; very heavy showers in the afternoon but a fine evening. High wind in the night."

But Constable's poetic fragments did not always succeed in achieving the synthesis of natural elements which he wished to show in a single painting. He found it difficult to express himself on a single canvas. Often, in fact, besides preparatory sketches, he used to express the same idea in two complementary but independent versions. From this time, he decided to plan his paintings more thoroughly. He prepared a draft of the same dimensions as the finished canvas, a full-size study which sometimes appeared more daring than the final version, especially in the application of the paint and the actual representation of the scene. This gives these studies a nearly modern air - or at least makes them more interesting to modern critics.

The full-size study for *The Hay Wain,* still in existence, was exhibited in Paris in 1824. Here the chiaroscuro (light and dark contrasted) with the sun illuminating places in the meadows in the background, the movement of the clouds and the rushing of the water produce feelings of immediacy and sincerity. The painting attracted some criticism for its unorthodox form and colours, its informal air and its lack of proper re- spect for perspective. But the main criticism of *The Hay Wain* at the time was for its alleged lack of idealism and elegance, so markedly in contrast with more fashionable paintings.

FAME IN FRANCE, NEGLECT IN ENGLAND

"**N**othing is clearly defined in the works of this painter and the subjects themselves are badly drawn. It is impossible to identify the type of tree represented, where their outlines start and finish. His skies are sullied with greys and his waters are sheets of ice not yet scratched by skates", wrote an anonymous critic in the *Revue Critique Des Productions De Peinture, Sculpture, Gravure Exposées Au Salon de 1824.* But he was out of tune with many of his compatriots at the time, who were finding in English painting - suddenly accessible after the long years of the Napoleonic wars - a revelation totally different from the marmoreal classicism of Ingres, by then the dominant French painter.

Constable's works in particular (especially his sketches and studies) had a profound influence on French Romantic painters such as Géricault, the young Delacroix and the landscape painters who would form the Barbizon School in the 1840s. But the insular Constable seems to have been rather indifferent to his fame in France; it was his continued lack of fame in England which concerned him. He constantly strove to perfect the execution of his paintings. He corrected the perspective, gave his figures a more finished look and removed and added details to produce a more balanced harmony in his pictures. These may all have been valid improvements in order to please the critics, but Constable apparently did not see that in making these refinements his finished paintings were losing much of their spontaneity and strength.

Looking at *The Glebe Farm* (page 26) painted about 1827, it is clear that the composition in the full-scale study is freer and less rigid than the finished piece. The study, with its use of chiaroscuro, and blue and yellow rather than green tones seems to be much truer than the definitive work which was "painted up" to satisfy his critics.

At the height of his career, when he had achieved some fame and success, Constable went to live in Brighton. He was not really inspired by the sea, but he painted the beach, the stormy skies and the brilliant golden-white light of a morning after the rain. These paintings meant little to him but some of the Brighton works are among his most original.

Constable produced his last works in Salisbury between 1828 and 1829. Many of these show the same views. In *Salisbury Cathedral From The Meadows,* among his last dramatic canvases, the care lavished on the details almost harms the unity of the composition. Certain details (which are not actually in Salisbury at all) seem remarkably familiar. These are memories of his dear Suffolk, such as the hay wagon which can once more be seen crossing the ford for the last time. *Old Sarum* (page 2) is a darker reworking of an early topic. Most dramatic of all is probably *The Cenotaph,* exhibited in 1836. This was a much stormier revision of an earlier version of 1823. Although the actual Cenotaph commemorated Sir Joshua Reynolds, the picture could almost stand as Constable's own memorial, for he died the next year.